Journaling has ~~been a strong part~~
of my life.

Why do I journal?

What is importance and life
changing outcome of journaling?

When I was about four years old I
use to mimic my great-
grandmother Blanca, she use to sit
for hours on her special recliner
reading, and writing. At the young
age I didn't really comprehend
what she was doing but whatever
it was I loved it.

I sat alongside of her with my own
notebook and scribbled trying to

really grasp her inspirational ways.

It wasn't until I was in school that I learned what she was doing. Grand-mother Blanca was the smartest and most precious women I have ever met. She taught herself new words with her own dictionary that she created by adding words and their definitions. She journaled her feelings and life stories and I yearn to know what was written. My favorite past time was sitting with her as she described her childhood or her days in the Old Cuba. When I was in middle school I started to journal it was my way out, journaling kept me sane through those tough teenage years. What my parents could not answer my journal took in.

How many of you can say you have your written words, stories, from when you were in school?

Probably not many, but why am I so fond of journaling?

My great-grandmother Blanca passed when I was fifteen and her daughter was cleaning out her stuff and threw away all her works.

I had no stories no memories just some pictures and jewelry but the prize her life encounters were in the garbage never to be seen. Though I was young I was a very strong minded child with a loud voice and I was upset that I had lost all her words and memories.

I decided I would write my own journals for records of my life journey.

Maybe when I pass my kids will throw my words away too or maybe they will pass them on to my own grand-daughters and their children.

Whatever the maybe outcome is I have found that people respect the dead. Once you pass others want to know you and especially those you love.

WHY? I can't really explain right now except we are simply curious.

BUT WHAT DOES THIS HAVE TO DO WITH the 30day challenge?

Stay with me I'll get there.

I started journaling when I was fourteen; and at 41 I have over five boxes filled with journals and life memories. Favorites my pregnancy journals, what I felt, what occurred, the dreams I had. I get to revisit all those passages of my life.

Today I journal, signs that I receive, times I spend with my family and my beautiful grand girls. The truth is everything goes in my journals.

One of the most precious things about journaling is wishing or asking for something and then getting the desire and witnessing that you asked for it and got it.

I will never forget when I prayed for a beautiful healthy baby girl, I already had two boys and I wanted to have all my children before I turned thirty. I was 25 at the time and I said if I don't have another child before my 29 birthday then I wasn't meant to have any more children but please oh please I want my baby girl. I asked for her in my journal of 1999 and my beautiful daughter was born in 2002.

THAT is what I call recording a passage of life.

****

****

Why the 30 day challenge is so important?

In life we must have regimens, rituals, habits that we can create and follow to lead a more successful life.

When I read the super beings and the abundance Book by Randolph Price he expressed how studies indicated that to start a ritual and make it part of your daily regimen you must do it for at the very least 21 days.

Working with many of you one on one I have noticed a recurring habit, you lack patience because you ask for something, you think about for maybe a week and then your upset because it's not there.

YOU must ALLOW! That is so important and this journey will teach you to allow, having patience, to schedule yourself.

Let's say you are taking these 30 days to lose ten pounds. Notice how I just said ten. Every day you will get an affirmation, a quote, and a burst of energy from the videos, or the meditations I create specifically to keep you on your journey.

Every day you try something new to add to your desire of dropping those ten pounds, and even if one day you fall off the wagon and decide you're going to have a chocolate brownie it's okay because you are going to make it. After all you just have to lose ten pounds. The key is to create a journey that is realistic for you, not GOD or source energy. Something you know you will be able to do, the best part is you can do as many of these 30 days challenges to lose the entire (let's say) fifty pounds you have to actually lose.

See how we didn't overwhelm you. See GOD will manifest anything you desire source energy is omnipresent within all, infinite we are the ones that hold ourselves back.

****

It's about creating simplicity through doing a little at a time until you are comfortable enough to add more.

****

What if you want to start your very own work from home business and you decided today you will have this business in thirty days.

Perfect, then you will start with your goal and your desire, and then you will add details you will start your business in thirty days time.

That will be your main focus not worry about clients, time or anything else. All you are doing is starting your business.

That was actually one of my 30day challenges.

I launched a store and campaign for my daughter in one for the 30 day challenges.

Then your next 3o day challenge can be marketing or getting 5 new clients.

Are you grasping this? SMALL SCOOPS....

You see; our main failure is we tend to want something BIG and that's wonderful BUT the issue is we overwhelm ourselves and then we procrastinate followed by every excuse in the book.

THIS way you will follow and you will act because you are adding a few grains of sand and soon you will have your beach.

****

When I first decided to come out of the spiritual closet and start my own business it was a bit scary.

I almost talked myself out of it before I even started.

I can write so many books on how my business would not work but I only needed one plan to make it work.

It all happened like miracle, from receiving the tools I needed to get clients after clients without even trying.

Don't get me wrong I am always working even when I am not social media active I am still working.

The best part if once I have you as a client I have you forever, WHY because I don't see you as clients I never have. I see everyone as my friends helping each other out. That is what I do? I create online friends that refer me to their friends and their families. Today my first clients are so not my clients though some just send me money because they feel they owe me. I don't charge them because they are my friends and they are always there for me too. They feel gratitude for all I do from my videos to my books, this is why I kindly accept the rewards they gift me. Thank you always.

Kelly was one of my very first clients and now is a great friend; though we lives states from each other she has helped me more than I have helped her.

When my son and his family went to live in South Carolina Kelly would send them winter Clothes because it's never cold here in Miami Florida.

She is constantly thinking about me and my family and I have her and her beautiful son in my daily prayers, we are more than friends we are family.

****

Journaling creates that because you input in your journals your life, your journey, your gratitude, and when you come back to your journals through the months and even years you see how much you have grown, the desires that have manifested. The patterns you break because since you journaled them you know not to repeat.

●●

Now that I have expressed a little about the POWER of journaling through a personal eye let's get to it. Each Day we will have specific affirmations, quotes, exercise, the energy and prayers of the day, to be followed by the video series in YouTube. I will add the title of each day for you to sequence.

You must send me your email if you purchase the book through Amazon so I can send you the private mediations just for the 30 day challenge.

****Un-Blocking the soul

****Un-Leashing your true potential

****Connecting with your soul energy

****Un-locking your true potential

****Un-blocking your past traumas

****Cutting chords

****Connecting with your spiritual guides

****Manifesting your truest desires

No matter where you find yourself you can repeat the mediations as you feel you need to, I will add them to specific days but repeat as often as you'd like, there is no wrong way to adding the extra mediations. NOW enjoy and be honest with yourself after all this is your journal, and your 30 day challenge, you don't need to do this for anyone but yourself, you don't need to prove anything to anyone but you. Do this for you and only you and watch as the world simply opens up in front of your very eyes.

************************** **********

DAY 1 of the 30 day challenge: A day of cleansing, relaxing, rejoicing with the energy of nature; to co-create with Source Energy. Today you start GRAND JOURNEY congratulations. Today you have made the decision of what will be next in your life. On the next few pages detail-fully express "yourself". I will ask very specific questions and the answers are all in your hands.

How are you feeling right now?

_____

_____

_____

_____

_____

_____

_____

_____

_____

_____

Why do you feel this way? What occurred, what was the situation, fully express if it was a positive feeling or even a negative one, express yourself.

_____

_____

_____

_____

_____

_____

_____

_____

_____

_____

_____

_____

_____

_____

**If your response was of letting go
you will start with the meditation**

to un-blocking your past trauma. This will free you and cut and un-block you from this specific situation. THEN when you finish come back to the goal setting. You want to be fully restored and cleared of that situation. If your response was a positive one let's start.

What are your intentions, your goal, for this 30day challenge? Take your time and be clear, specific, and add details._____

_____

_____

_____

_____

What will this goal do for you when you manifest it? How will you feel once you have completed this intention and it is right in your Now moment?

NOW go watch the DAY one video before the next step.

****

****

Take this area to express what you are grateful for NOW at this very moment in your life?

_____

_____

_____

_____

_____

Be grateful for the goal express your gratitude over this intention as if it was already in your Now moment.

_____

_____

_____

_____

_____

_____

_____

_____

_____

_____

_____

_____

_____

_____

As you move through your day
ONE energy your affirmation will
be "WITH GOD ANYTHING AND
EVERYTHING IS POSSIBLE" You can
add your God, your saints, your
angels, your personal belief.

Continue expressing gratitude if
you need more
space._____

_____

_____

_____

_____

_____

_____

_____

_____

_____

_____

_____

_____

_____

_____

_____

_____

_____

Day two: Today you will daydream; today what your

teacher probably scolded you for in school you are allowed to do all day LONG.

On the next few pages write out a very detailed vision of your intention, goal, desire, dream...

But there is a twist you will write it in present time, as if you are journaling something that already occurred, like a vivid memory.

Go with it allow it to flow, and watch your Day 2 video. Then you will adorn this Journal with images of your visions. Print them out, maybe use your phone to take pictures add yourself in the images. It is very important you create this vision as a memory as if it has already occurred.

"Look around less, imagine more."

Esther Hicks

EverydayPowerBlog.com

http://everydaypowerblog.com/2015/09/16/25-inspirational-esther-hicks-quotes-on-manifesting-your-dreams/

_____

_____

_____

_____

_____

_____

You are doing beautifully your simply awesome.

_____

_____

_____

_____

_____

_____

_____

_____

_____ As you close this day two right before bed close your eyes and continue your day-dream as you dose off. Add your favorite spiritual music to really uplift and inspire your visions. Sweet dreams._____

_____

_____

_____

_____

_____

_____

_____

_____

_____

_____

_____

_____

_____

_____

_____

_____

_____

_____

_____

_____

Day 3 Action: WOW you are already in day 3. You are so awesome; you will do this entire challenge.

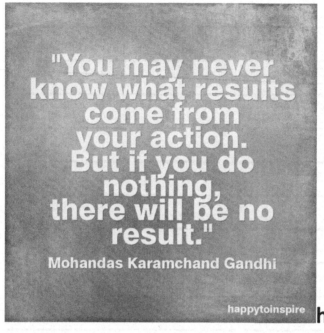

"You may never know what results come from your action. But if you do nothing, there will be no result."

Mohandas Karamchand Gandhi

happytoinspire

ht
tp://www.marikoworld.com/quot
es/action-quotes/

Prioritize an action plan, organize yourself, set up your pintables, or write them in this journal. Set appointments for your goals and desires. Organize personally your appointments "for you" and you only. Create by day by week, and by the closing of this thirty day challenge.

How do you feel, you are on day 3. What has been occurring? Simply write anything and everything that comes to your mind.

_____

_____

_____

_____

_____

_____

_____

_____

_____

MON.	TUES.	WED.	THURS.	FRI.	SAT.	SUN.

Goals, Intentions, desires,

Major

Goal:_____

_____

_____

_____

_____

_____

_____

_____

Outcome:

_____

_____

_____

_____

_____

_____

DAY 4: "I am at one with Source energy". Affirm all day as you go through your day four. Refocus your energy from any negative thoughts by affirming.

Watch Day 4 video: Walk the gratitude walk and before bed write below praise to yourself. Details of your refocusing and by allowing source energy to flow anything that opened up for you today.

_____

_____

_____

_____

_____

_____

_____

_____

_____

_____

_____

_____

_____

_____

_____

_____

_____Before you
go to bed connect with Archangel
Jophiel and ask her to replenish
the Love energy within you, good
night._____

_____

_____

_____

_____

_____

_____

_____

_____

_____

_____

_____

_____

_____

_____

_____

_____

_____

_____

_____

_____

_____

_____

_____

Day 5: the energy of today is WATER, to allow the energy of water to cleanse and clear you.

Take a sea-salt bath or shower right before you close the day and do the meditation "Cutting Chords".

Relax connect with peace and affirm.

I AM PEACE.

I am peaceful. Write down all that brings peace in your life below. What peaceful moments are you grateful for?

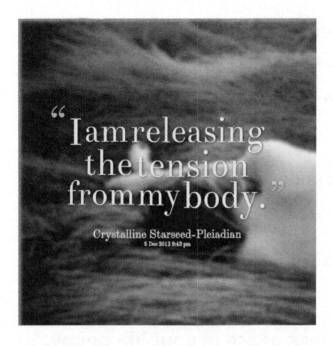

"I am releasing the tension from my body."

Crystalline Starseed-Pleiadian
5 Dec 2012 9:48 pm

http://www.quotationof.com/rel
easing.html

_____

_____

_____

_____

_____

_____

Day 6: Enjoy the energy of praise today; give yourself PRAISE because you are doing amazing work. As you watch Day 6 allow and invite the archangels Michael and Raziel to enfold you with spiritual connection. I added pictures of the archangels here to connect with the beautiful energies. Today is extremely special because it is the beginning of connecting with your guides to receiving messages.

Connect outdoors under the SUN and within nature to speak and allow Archangel Raziel to send you signs and messages. SIMPLY relax and enjoy what comes through be open. You can do the "Connecting with your spiritual guides meditation" to invoke the energy.

In the next few pages I will add some spiritual quotes for you to affirm as you go through today. Inviting Archangel Michael to protect and enfold your spiritual 30day challenge journey. BE open as you never know what Archangel Raziel will show you. This will be amazing write it all down.

Spiritual Nature

messages:_____

_____

_____

_____

_____

_____

_____

_____

_____

_____

_____

_____

_____

_____

_____

_____

Dor

een Virtue's Archangel Cards.

_____

_____

_____

_____

_____

_____

_____

_____

_____

_____

_____

_____

_____

_____

_____

_____

_____

_____

_____

Praise
yourself:_____

_____

_____

_____

_____

_____

_____

_____

_____

_____

_____

_____

When you did your connecting
with your spiritual guides
meditation what images,
thoughts, messages or anything
in-between did you
receive?_____

_____

_____

_____

_____

_____

_____

_____

Pray for the protection and shielding of Archangel Michael as I continue to do so through the next few days and weeks.

_____

_____

_____

Cleaning table:
Clean Closets:
Clean closed spaces: **Cabinets** **Under beds** **Drawers**
Dust HOME: **Dust under sofa's** **Spider webs:** **Under furniture:** **Over furniture:**
Throw away all broken items or repair them

Clothes
Underwear
Socks
Pillows
Sheets
Anything broken or ripped or torn.

THIS is part of the FLOW to create a cleansed feeling in your home; this doesn't have to be done in one sitting you are simply clearing away to allow the energy of receiving.

I created the above organized list so you can highlight or check marks as you go through the cleansing process. I speak more of this on Day 13.

Take your time and do a task a day.

_____

_____

_____

_____

_____

_____

_____

_____

_____

_____

_____

_____

_____

_____

_____

_____

_____

_____

_____

_____

Day 7: "*Our God specializes in working through normal people who believe in a supernormal God who will do his work through them*". *Bruce Wilkinson*

Congratulations its day 7 you have just completed an entire week. Today you are fearless because you accomplished a major goal you have completed 7 days. Today is simple allow, connect with peace and feel the presence of your angelic team. Allow your angels to guide you, connect with Archangel Michael who is protecting you and guiding you forward.

_____

_____

_____

_____

_____

_____

_____

_____

_____

_____

_____

_____

_____

_____

_____

_____

_____

_____

_____

_____

_____

_____

_____

_____Look for the signs, what did you receive:_____

http://angels.about.com/od/AngelsReligiousTexts/f/How-Does-Angel-Michael-Represent-Hod-Glory-On-Kabbalah-S-Tree-Of-Life.htm

_____

_____

_____

_____

_____

_____

_____

_____

_____

_____

_____

_____

_____

_____

_____

_____

_____

_____

_____

Day 8: "Sometimes letting go is an act of a far greater power than defending or holding on". Eckhart Tolle.

Today's energy is to simply LET go. That means you detach yourself from what is holding you back. Example: I was attached to my old home, no matter what I did, how I prayed I could not seem to detach myself from its hold. I wrote a letter to my home saying thanks for taking me and my family in but it was time for us to say our goodbyes and I went outside and burnt the letter. Allowed myself to fully reconcile with the house and I renounced its grip and power over me. I simply said in a peaceful tone GOODBYE.

TODAY you will simply LET go, your choice you can say it out loud maybe in front of the mirror or write a dear letter. However you choose simply let it go, connect with peace.

I will give you an open area to LET go, to release your feelings.

What is holding you back?

Why do you feel this has taken your power?

What should you do to let go?

Allow your mind to set those feelings free, write out all that comes to your mind. This is your journal express yourself. BE truthful; be honest with you because right now you matter very much.

This is why you are doing this challenge. This is why you are taking the time and energy because you matter very much.

Allow and LET

GO_____

_____

_____

_____

_____

_____

_____

_____

_____

_____

_____

_____

_____

_____

_____

_____Allow,_____

_____

_____

_____

_____

_____

_____

_____

_____

_____

_____

_____

_____

_____Let

go_____

_____

_____

_____

_____

_____

_____

_____

_____

_____

_____

breathe_____

_____

_____

_____

_____

_release_____

_____

_____

_____

_____

_____

_____

_____

_____

_____

_____

_____

_____

_____

_____

_____

_____before you go to

bed on this day 8 simply allow gratitude to fill you and do a meditation your choice. Allow yourself to be guided to one of the meditation and I'll see you in the morning.

Day 9 "Gifts from God" Pay attention to what is occurring

today. Have you received anything in the past 8 days? Be open be aware and open your arms to receiving.

Today is the day you fully connect with your angels. Today you will ask.

What questions do you want your angels to answer? Go ahead write them below and leave room after each question to write out the answers as they are reveled throughout the day.

BE OPEN

Question

1)_____

_____

_____

_____

_____allow_____

_____Question

2)_____

_____

_____

_____

_____

_____

_____

_____

_____

_____

_____

_____

_____

_____

_____

_____

_____

_____

_____

_____

_____

_____

_____

_____

_____all

ow space to come back when the
questions are answered
sometimes the arrival of the
answer is divinely guided. DO not
push anything let the answers find
you._____

Day 10 "To believe deeply that GOD is present and at work in human life is to understand that I am a beloved child of this Father and hence, free to trust. That makes a profound difference in the way I relate to myself and others; it makes an enormous difference in the way I live".

Brennan Manning

LOVE is the energy of the day.
What do you
LOVE?_____

_____

_____

_____

_____

_____

_____

_____

_____

_____

_____

_____

_____

_____

do you need more LOVE In your life?_____

_____

_____

_____

_____

_____

_____

_____

_____

_____

_____

_____

_____

_____

_____

_____

_____

_____

_____

_____

_____

_____Are you
connected with God Source
energy?_____

_____

_____

_____
_____ Do
you feel LOVE when you are
connected?_____

_____

_____

_____

_____

_____

_____

_____

_____

_____

_____

_____

_____

_____Where or
why do you feel
disconnection?_____

_____

_____

_____

_____

_____

_____

_____

_____

___Where or why do you feel lack
in
LOVE?_____

_____

_____

_____

_____

_____

_____

_____

_____

_____

_____

_____

_____

_____

_____

_____

_____Do this tonight with time "mediate" with Archangel Jophiel connecting with LOVE energy frequency to align the heart chakra; by becoming RECEPTIVE to LOVE. Then below all thoughts, messages, anything that flowed ad you did this meditation. THEN go to sleep and focus on a beautiful PINK light that surrounds you and engulfs your very essence, the LOVE energy from God source through archangel Jophiel and onto you.

_____

_____

_____

_____

_____

_____

_____

_____

_____

_____

_____

_____

_____

_____

_____ Be

expressive _____

_____

_____

_____

_____

_____

_____

_____

_____

_____

_____

_____

_____

_____

_____

_____

_____Who did
you
see?_____

_____

_____

_____

_____

_____

_____

_____

_____

_____

_____

_____

_____

_____

_____What
did you
feel?_____

_____

_____

_____

http://www.clearandconnect.com
/angel-meditations/attunement-
with-archangel-jophiel-patron-
saint-of-artists

_____

_____

_____

_____

_____

_____

_____

_____

_____

**DAY 11 "SAT....CHIT....ANANDA....
=Follow your Bliss.**

"FOLLOW YOUR BLISS and don't be afraid and doors will open before you where there were no doors". Joseph Campbell

Do the open the doors meditation (morning or midday) for best results. As you move into the day repeat ...SAT...CHIT...ANANDA..... You are a beautiful soul you are perfect, you are BLISS energy. Simply walk through your day as

your darken room is Now fully lit and your doors are fully open. Express below your thoughts and feelings, allow the energy of the beautiful angels to guide you through this day of BLISS.....

Watch as your energy is no longer in the same frequency as those you are surrounded by. Your energy is NOW a higher energy and you are connected with BLISS. SAT...CHIT...ANANDA..._____

_____

_____

_____

_____

_____

_____

_____

_____

_____

_____

_____

_____

_____

_____

_____

_____

_____before
you go to bed, repeat
SAT….CHIT….ANANDA…. repeat as
you fall asleep when you awaken
below write any messages,
dreams, visions that you may have
encountered._____

_____

_____

_____

_____

_____

_____

_____

_____

_____

_____

_____

_____

_____

_____

_____

Day 12 Oh I love today!!!!! Today
you will get a beautiful post card
or a letter note, some nice
stationary because this letter is
for you. This note you are writing

is for Future "YOU". Make it beautiful.

In this note express just how proud you are to future you.

Example: Dear "me" I am so very proud of you because (and express all the reasons you are so proud, be honest and very loving, like you are writing this letter to someone true and dear to your heart. YOU are because you are TRUE and you are DEAR). Then express the experience of co-creating the intention, desire, goal you started this journey with. Fill the note with gratitude (because you know it is already yours). Write this letter as if you were writing to a distant friend you love and sharing this wonderful experience and you are so grateful and proud of all the accomplishments this dear friend achieved. SEAL the letter and date it to be opened exactly 30 days from today's date. You can put the letter in your journal or in a sacred place. I like to see mine everyday because as the days pass you will not remember what was written and you will be curious but don't let curiosity get the better hand open on the date intended.

HOW did it feel writing to yourself_____

_____

_____

_____

_____

_____

_____

_____

_____

_____

_____

_____

_____

_____

_____

_____

_____Did you
have any signs or messages
today?_____

_____

_____

_____

_____

_____

_____

__Before bed, what are you grateful for today?_____

_____

_____

_____

_____

_____

_____

_____

_____

_____

_____

_____

_____

Day 13 "O Divine Providence, I ask not for more riches, but more wisdom with which to make wiser use of the riches you gave me at birth, consisting in the power to control and direct my own mind to whatever ends I might desire". Napoleon Hill

Today is special (you will hear me repeat that often) today you will write your intention, goals, and or desires and you will add a twist.

WHAT ARE YOU OFFERING IN EXCHANGE for this DESIRE?

Example: better health I am offering a higher vibration to uplift the human energy.

BUCKLE UP our journey starts to intensify NOW and further through our days together.

Directions for today: re-write the quote above below in your writing followed by your intentions desire goals and the offering for this request.

Then throughout the day read the quote 12 times. You can re-write on a smaller paper to keep the quote near._____

_____

_____

DAY 14 "The best and most beautiful things in the world cannot be seen or even touched they must be felt with the heart". Helen Keller

LOVE is the equation of everything. I often find myself in a repetitive state when there is a bumpy road I have encountered. "ONLY LOVE IS REAL".

THAT is your focus today, when you find yourself next to someone or something negative; repeat the mantra.

ONLY LOVE is real....

NOW as only LOVE is real is the energy of the day. Get a beautiful sheet of paper something that sparks your interest and write out your goal, intention, and desire.

THEN decorate your paper after your done writing out your intention, goals and or desire. Maybe add some perfume or soft scented oils. KEEP this paper with you all day, pull out often and read it, then say BY closing your eyes.

ONLY LOVE IS REAL.....

Repeat 12 times throughout the day.

What feelings rose today?_____

What emotions have you been encountering and how did they make you
feel?_____

_____

_____

_____

_____

_____

_____

_____

_____

_____

_____

_____

_____

_____

_____

_____

_____

_____

_____

_____

_____

_____

_____

_____

_____

Day 15 CONGRATULATIONS you just hit the halfway mark!!!!!!

https://healthplane.com/metatrons-cube/

"It's not how much we give but how much love we put into giving." Mother Teresa

What have you given in the past fifteen

days?_____

_____

_____

_____

_____

_____

_____

_____

_____

_____

_____

_____

_____**This is
not a test, there is not right or
wrong. This is for you; an exercise**

to get you to think about the high frequency energy of GIVING.

Message from archangel Metatron, one of the lessons he taught when we walked the earth as Enoch. "In life there are orders a sequence that is to be followed for balance, when you are out of balance it is because you are not following the order. Giving as for receiving is part of that divine order. If you are asking you must give, what are you giving for that which you have been asking? It is a simple mathematical solution 1+1=2 2-1=1 As you move through today's energy I am giving you a piece to the puzzle of life enjoy your creative expression through the law of giving." Metatron.

Yesterday we wrote out or intention, goal, desire, and today repeating yesterday exercise you will write what you are offering in return for your receiving.

Ask archangel Metatron anything you would like to know, keep it simple if you are new with your angels.

_____

_____

_____

_____

_____

_____

_____

_____

_____

_____

_____

_____

_____

_____

_____

_____

_____Mantra: I can do anything I set my mind to._____

_____

_____

_____

_____

_____

_____

_____

_____

Day 16: Beautiful day isn't it?

**"Ask and it will be given to you."
Mathew 7:7**

**On a small post it note you will
write out the above bible verse,
then you will put your intention
paper with your giving paper and
unite all three with a ribbon. You
can add wax to seal the beautiful
work you have just completed in
three shorts days. Put this note in
your sacred place or even in the
bible within the verse above.**

Allow your intuition to guide you.

What messages or emotions can today?_____

_____

_____

_____

_____

_____

_____

_____

_____

_____

_____

_____

_____

_____

_____

_____

_____

_____

_____

_____Are you
feeling better or is something
lacking? Express your true
emotions._____

_____

_____

_____

_____

_____

_____

_____

_____

_____

_____

_____

_____

_____

_____

_____

_____

Day 17: "If you believe you will receive." Mathew 21:22

Today you will celebrate, go out for tea; invite some friends over you are celebrating your spiritual union with the angels. You are celebrating the manifestation of your goal, intention, desire.

In order to receive you must believe, in order to believe you must play the part of already

having achieved. Therefore CELEBRATE!!!!

Angel messages:_____

_____

_____

_____

_____

_____

_____

_____

_____**signs**_____

_____

_____

_____

_____

_____

_____visions_____

_____

_____

_____

_____

_____

_____

_____

_____dreams

_____

_____

_____

_____

Day 18 "Answers come to me in my dreams" Raziel

Today we will be visiting the angelic realm with beautiful Lisa Beachy **"Visit the Angelic Realm & meet your Angel**

Meditation Video" YouTube video title.

Take your time when doing this meditation as you want to be relaxed so you can enjoy the full affect.

Write down what you experienced.

_____

_____

_____

_____

_____

_____

_____

_____

_____

_____

_____

_____

_____

_____
_____
_____
_____
_____
_____
_____
_____
_____

Day 19 Arch Angel Ariel is guiding you and your prosperity and courage to prosper.
Ariel is the beautiful feminine energy angel that brings great news of prosperity and her energy is strong on DAY 18.
She wants to align you with your financial career and inflow of abundance; also with the courage to fulfill your divine purpose.
Today your energy will shift with the courage of acting upon your prosperity.

What is your purpose?_____

_____

_____

_____

_____

_____

_____

_____

_____

_____

_____

_____What do you feel
is your
purpose?_____

_____

_____

_____

_____

_____

_____

_____

_____

_____

_____

_____

_____

_____

_____

_____

_____

_____

_____When you were a child and were asked. "What do you want to do or be when you grow up; what was your answer?_____

_____

_____

_____

_____

_____

_____

_____

_____

_____

_____Are you doing
and or living your divine
purpose?_____

_____

_____

_____

_____

_____

_____

_____

_____

_____

_____

_____

_____

_____

_____

_____

_____

_____

_____

_____

_____

_____

_____

_____

_____

_____and if you are not
explain why, express what
changes you can make to act
upon this purpose. This is
your truth. Be
expressive._____

_____

_____

_____

_____

_____

_____

_____

_____

_____

_____

_____

_____DECLARE: From this day forward (write out the specific date) I declare I will (and write out what your action steps are towards living your purpose._____

_____

_____

_____

_____

_____

_____

_____

_____

_____

_____

_____

_____

_____

_____

_____

_____

_____

_____

_____

_____

_____

_____

_____

_____

_____

_____

_____

_____

_____

_____

**Day 20 "The greatest pleasure
in life is doing what others
say you cannot do".**

Today we continue our courage and prosperity journey with beautiful Archangel Ariel.

Today you will sit in a quiet place where you will invite archangel Ariel and ask her a specific question and you will ask her to send a CLEAR message.

Question_____

_____
_____
_____
_____
_____
_____
_____
_____
_____
_____

Answer_____

_____**Has your goal,**

intention, or desire shifted in any way?_____

_____

_____

_____

_____

_____

_____

_____

_____

_____

_____

_____

_____

_____

_____

_____

_____**What**

has happened since your meditation with the angelic realm, what signs, messages have entered your life?_____

_____

_____

_____

_____

_____

_____

_____

_____

_____

_____

_____

_____

_____

_____

_____

_____

_____

_____

_____

_____

_____

_____

_____

_____

_____

_____

_____

_____

Day 21
Happy end of week three.
"BREATHE it's all OKAY"
Sometimes we push too hard
and we want this without even
expecting anything will occur.
TODAY the energy is all is
well, all is just fine, everything
is okay.

THIS is the end of your third week.
TODAY you rest; you can do a meditation of choice or simply sit in nature and write what comes.
Allow, Allow , allow…..

_____

_____

_____

_____

_____

_____

_____

_____

_____

_____

_____

_____

_____

_____

_____

_____

_____

_____

_____

_____

_____

_____

_____

_____

_____

_____

_____

_____

_____

_____

_____

_____

_____

Day 22 "As you start to walk out on the way, the way appears." Rumi

Congratulations this is your last week of the 30 days you have ritually acted upon your true desires.
HOW DO YOU FEEL?_____

_____

_____

_____

_____

_____

_____

_____

_____

_____

_____

_____

_____

_____

_____

_____

_____

_____

_____

_____

_____

_____

_____What
have you accomplished or
feel
accomplished?_____

_____

_____

_____

_____

_____

_____

_____

_____

_____

_____

_____

_____

_____

_____

_____

_____

_____

_____What are you grateful for?_____

_____

_____

_____

_____

_____

_____

_____

_____

_____

_____

_____

_____

_____

_____

_____

_____

_____

_____

_____

Today's exercise (on your time day or night) go outside and ask for what you want?

_____

_____

_____

_____

_____

_____

_____

_____

_____

_____

_____

_____

_____

_____

_____

_____

_____

_____

_____

_____

Day 23

I will not let anyone walk through my mind with their dirty feet.
- gandhi

"I will not let anyone walk

through my mind with dirty feet." Ganhdi
https://www.lindajferguson.com/2013/10/

Your mind is sacred as is your life believing in you is all it takes. It matters not what others want of you or for you. All that matter is what you want?

Today you start planning HOW you will achieve this goal, intention, and desire, no matter what you are asking of by this time signs have manifested. You have had dreams, confirmations, visions, intuitive messages, books, media, no matter the venue the signs have been there.

In the next few pages I added organization for you to do 5 things towards achieving your wanting.

FROM today forward you will do 5 different things towards your wanting.

Let's start with researching. A great way to connect and allow the creative flow is with beautiful archangel Jophiel and in nature. Archangel Jophiel is always easy to talk to in nature, go outside and write out your plan.

WHAT did you receive in your outdoors experience with archangel Jophiel?_____

_____

_____

_____

_____

_____

_____

"Five action steps toward your GOAL, INTENTION, DESIRE."
No matter what you are aiming at taking inspirational steps is the way to manifestation.
Steps

Results

Use this table as reference, set 5 action plans. 5 tasks you will do towards this wanting. Examples if you are losing weight what five things can you do to achieve this?

If you are writing a book what five different things can you take action on to achieve this?

_____

_____

_____

_____

_____

_____

_____

Day 24 "You are joy looking for a way to express." Esther Hicks

Busy day, fun joyful filled with experience; today you will do all five tasks and create a special relationship harmony time.

In order to multi-task and organize and prioritize you have to be assertive and this is always the tough part. When we really want to say no but we always say yes. You will look at that today as you plan out your tasks and your special time.
BE creative, have fun, and do it with joy. No stress there is

no wrong just allow yourself
to do the very best you can
do.
It is all about repetition and
practice.

_____

_____

_____

_____

_____

_____

_____

5 action steps towards you're wanting.

Action

Results

Day 25 "Reality is built out of thought, and our every thought begins to create reality."
Edgar Cayce.

Oh what a fun day, today is a cut and paste day. Do you remember your kindergarten days when you would cut out pictures and paste them?

That is what you will do today.
BE creative, find pictures, clippings that bring JOY, and fill you with HAPPINESS. Maybe they resemble what you are wanting. Maybe it's puppies.
"Pictures that bring out the very best in you."
I will allow room for your thought writing and you can add your clippings around the next pages.

_____

_____

_____

_____

_____

_____

_____

_____

_____

_____

_____

_____

_____

_____

_____

_____

_____

_____

_____

_____

_____

_____

_____

_____

_____

_____How

are you feeling today?

_____

_____

_____

_____

_____

_____

_____

_____

_____

_____

_____

_____

_____

_____Any signs, or messages?_____

_____

_____

_____

_____

_____

_____

_____

_____

_____

_____

_____

_____

_____

_____

_____

_____

_____

_____

_____

_____

_____

_____ideas,
inspirations,_____

_____

_____

_____

_____

_____

_____

_____

_____

_____

_____

_____

_____

_____

_____

_____

_____

_____

_____

_____

_____

_____

_____What are
you feeling gratitude
over?_____

_____

_____

_____
_____
_____
_____
_____
_____
_____
_____
_____
_____

Daily action plan

Action

Results				

Day 26
"Abundance is not something
we acquire. It is something we
tune into." Dr. Wayne Dyer

Wow are you proud of
yourself or what?
You are on day 26. Today
focus on a meditation that
resonates with your
emotions, with how you feel,
allow yourself to feel.
Archangel Jeremiel says to
you "Look how far you come,
look at how much you have
accomplished, and bask in
the full feeling. Resolve to
heal your life from this
moment on, make a habit of

tuning into the higher
vibration, and anything
unbalanced will slowly
dissolve."

Today review all go ahead,
was it worth your 30 days?
Why or why not be honest.

_____

_____

_____

_____

_____

_____

_____

_____

_____

_____

_____

_____

_____

_____

_____

_____

_____

_____

_____

_____

_____

_____

_____What
do you feel in this review of
your spiritual angelic
progress? What you truly
connected with your
angels?_____

_____

_____

_____

_____

_____

_____

_____

_____

_____

_____

_____

_____

_____

_____

_____

_____

_____

_____

_____

_____

_____

_____ask archangel
Jeremiel your
question?_____

_____

_____

_____

_____

_____

_____

_____

_____

_____

_____

_____

_____

_____

_____What is his
answer?_____

_____

_____

_____

_____

_____

_____

_____

_____

_____

_____

_____

_____

_____

_____

_____

_____

_____

_____

_____

_____

_____

_____

_____

_____

_____What is the result of
your life's review? Are you
happy in your life as of
today? What changes have
you experienced in these past

**26
days?**_____

_____

_____

_____

_____

_____

_____

_____

_____

_____

_____

_____

_____

_____

_____

_____

_____

_____

_____

_____

_____

_____

_____

_____allow your
emotions to flow over the
pages_____

_____

_____

_____

_____

_____

_____

_____

_____

_____

_____

_____

_____

Actions

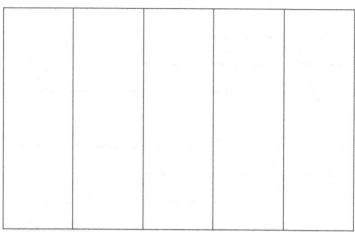

Results

Day 27 "Hold the vision TRUST the process" unknown author

We are almost there "YEAH". NOW today you will ground your energy with archangel Ariel. Go outside take off your shoes (pay attention where you stand) a grassy area, sand in the beach or water. Wherever you are grounding your-self Connect with Archangel Ariel by simply standing and allowing her to work the prosperity energy over you, allow, connect, and stand still. No wrong just allow your intuition to guide you.

WHAT did you feel after your grounding experience?

_____

_____

_____

_____

_____

_____

_____

_____

_____

_____

_____

_____

_____

_____

_____

_____-Did
you ask archangel Ariel anything?
Did you receive any
messages?_____

_____

_____

_____

_____

_____

_____

_____

_____

_____

_____

_____

_____

_____What are you grateful
for
today?_____

_____

_____

_____

_____

_____

_____

_____

_____

_____

_____

_____

_____

_____

_____

_____

_____

Five action steps

Action

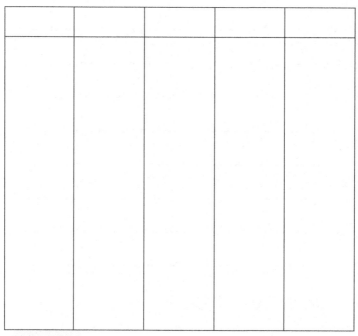

Results

Day 28 "I'm realistic I expect miracles." Dr. Wayne Dyer.

I love Dr. Dyer I still remember the first time I heard him on PBS I was so captivated and forever in love. That little quote or what I call an affirmation or mantra is so true if

you can just actually see it for what it is.

I'm realistic isn't that something our mothers and teacher would say when they wanted you off day dream land? Get off that cloud was my mom's favorite scolding to me.

MY belief I believe in miracles I see them daily. Just waking up each morning is a miracle and when you start to LIVE life that way; well that is what it's all about.

What miracles do you seek from this journey?_____

_____

_____

_____

_____

_____

_____

_____

_____

_____

_____

_____

_____Your at the end how do you
feel?_____

_____

_____

_____

_____

_____

_____

_____

_____

_____

_____

_____

_____

_____

_____

_____

_____What miracles have you experienced in your life?(anytime)_____

_____

_____

_____

_____

_____

_____

_____

_____

_____

_____

_____

_____

_____

_____

_____

_____

_____

_____Today
you will do an incantation out
loud like a true weirdo.

I am expecting a miracle, nothing
less than a miracle! Repeat it out

loud outdoors in the shower while you're doing your daily chores, your five daily action tasks.

REPEAT 12 times throughout this day.

Expect the unexpected from this day for this will be different from now on. YOU WILL EXPECT nothing less of a miracle in your life.

WAIT for this miracle with all your essence, feel it with every drop of your vitality.

NOW explore day 28 follow your intuition, what will you do today?_____

_____

_____

_____

_____

_____

_____

_____

_____

_____

_____

_____

_____

_____

_____

_____

_____What angel or
angels are around you today?
What have they said or shown
you? Any dreams,

visions?_____

_____

_____

_____

_____

_____

_____

_____

_____

_____

_____

_____

_____

_____

_____

_____

_____

_____

_____What are you filled with gratitude Over?_____

_____

_____

_____

_____

_____

_____

_____

_____

_____

_____

_____

_____

_____

_____

_____

_____

_____

Five action tasks

Action

Results

Notes

thoughts_____

_____

_____

_____

_____

Day 29 "You get there by realizing you are already there." Buddha

Do you understand that quote, you get there when you see, feel, touch, taste, hear, and know you are already there.

Today we call upon Archangel Michael to enfold us with his divine energy of protection and

loving guidance as we continue this journey.

Archangel Ariel to fill us with courage and connect us with Divine prosperity.

Archangel Jeremiel to help us see all is already resolved and if it becomes too much to give it all over to him. RELEASE, LET GO, ALLOW..

To connect with archangel Raziel so we can manifest all we desire from our inner loving truthful divine beings and that from this new journey on we DECLARE to be BLISS and only BLISS.

Amen and so it is.

SIMPLY allow the flow of energy and thought you did it you are awesome. You manifest it all now._____

_____

_____

_____

_____

_____

_____

_____

_____

_____

_____

_____

_____

_____

_____

_____

_____

_____

_____

_____

_____

_____

_____

_____

_____

Five action Tasks

Action

Results

DAY 30 "All life is a manifestation of the spirit, the manifestation of Love." Morihei Ueshiba

Congratulation today is the day you have been waiting for but it will not be what you expect.

Today will be almost a complete repletion to your day one.

WHY because you are different you no longer are the beginner you are a bit wiser, more positive, more aligned and today when you set the same goal, intention, and desire, you will declare it with all your LOVE and your might.

YOU will move throughout this beautiful day 30 and say out loud you're wanting 12 times.

The last time will be right before you go to sleep like your prayer, even if you didn't pray before you will repeat your wanting, you will declare it and you will know on this 30th day of your spiritual journey with the beautiful angels of manifestation that it is already yours.

Amen and so it is.

What have you learned from this journaling with your angelic team experience?_____

_____

_____

_____

_____

_____

_____

_____

_____

_____

_____

_____

_____

_____

_____

_____

_____

_____

_____

_____

_____

_____

_____

_____Is this really your
last day or is this Just the

beginning of a beautiful spiritual journey? Why or why not?_____

_____

_____

_____

_____

_____

_____

_____

_____

_____

_____

_____

_____

_____

_____

"Time is more valuable than money. You can get more money but you cannot get more time."
Jim Rohn

_____

_____

_____

_____

_____

_____

_____

_____

_____

_____

_____

_____

_____

_____

_____

_____

_____

_____

_____Are you proud
of yourself? Why or why
not?_____

_____

_____

_____

_____

_____

_____

_____

_____

_____

_____

_____

_____

_____

_____

_____

_____

_____

_____

_____

_____

_____

_____

_____

_____

_____What have you changed in these past 30 days?_____

_____

_____

Five tasks

Action

Results

This is the beginning of a beautiful relationship with your angels use the next few pages to write anything you have experienced or would like to experience; any thoughts, visions, dreams, and or signs._____

_____

_____

_____

_____

_____

_____

_____

_____

_____

_____

_____

_____

_____

_____

_____

_____

_____

_____

_____

_____

_____**What's your angels names?**_____

_____

_____

_____

_____

_____

_____

_____

_____

_____How does your
angel looks or your angels energy
feel?_____

_____

_____

_____

_____

_____

_____

_____

_____

_____

_____

_____visions_____

_____
_____
_____
_____
_____
_____
_____
_____
_____
_____
_____
_____
_____
_____
_____
_____
_____Dreams

_____

_____

_____

_____

_____

_____

_____

_____

_____

_____LOVE_____

_____

_____

_____

_____

_____

_____

_____

_____

_____

_____

_____

_____

_____

_____

_____

_____

_____

_____thank

you_____

_____

_____

_____

_____

_____

_____

_____

_____

_____

_____

_____

_____

_____

_____

_____

_____

_____

_____

_____

_____

_____

_____As a

thank you for all my work and loving energy please leave and AMAZING 5 star review, share with your friends and family, or give as gifts, the universe blesses GIVERS always.

LOVE and LIGHT

Daisy

_____

_____

_____

_____

_____

_____

_____

_____

_____

For Videos and Meditations to go along with this amazing journaling experience go to my YouTube channel Daisyf1305 or email me at silvermist1305@yahoo.com to be a part of our secret angel group on Facebook.

Made in the USA
Columbia, SC
24 December 2020

27937046R00137